THE ULTIMATE
*NSYNC
QUIZ BOOK

THE ULTIMATE
*NSYNC
QUIZ BOOK

BY MAGGIE MARRON

MetroBooks

MetroBooks

An Imprint of the Michael Friedman Publishing Group, Inc.

Library of Congress Cataloging-in-Publication Data available upon request.

ISBN 1-58663-135-7

Editor: Dan Heend
Art Director: Kevin Ullrich
Designer: Kirsten Berger
Photo Editor: Jami Ruszkai
Production Manager: Rosy Ngo

Color separations by Bright Arts Graphics (S) Pte Ltd
Printed in the U.S.A. by R.R. Donnelley & Sons Co.

3 5 7 9 10 8 6 4 2

For bulk purchases and special sales, please contact:
Friedman/Fairfax Publishers
Attention: Sales Department
230 Fifth Avenue
New York, NY 10001
212/685-6610 FAX 212/685-3916

Visit our website:
www.metrobooks.com

Dedication

For Jake Ryan and Stephanie Rose

Acknowledgments

This book could not be possible without all the *NSYNC fans out there—thanks, guys, for sharing my undying love of these babes! And thanks to everyone who made this book possible, especially to Christine Guarino Mayer, who has become my right hand in collecting celebrity trivia. Without her, I could never have gotten all the juicy tidbits I used to make the quiz questions in this book. Let's not forget my editor, Dan Heend, for taking another chance on old Maggie! And finally, Francine Hornberger—thanks again for being such a great pop culture muse!

About the Author

A New York–based freelance writer and editor, Maggie Marron is the author of several pictorial celebrity biographies, including *Britney Spears: Stylin'*, *Ricky Martin*, *The Backstreet Boys*, *Will Smith: From Rap Star to Mega Star*, and *Christina Aguilera: The Unauthorized Biography* as well as *The Ultimate Backstreet Boys Quiz Book* and *The Ultimate Britney Spears Quiz Book*. She has also written for *Kickin'* magazine and profiled numerous celebrities for *People Magazine Online*. Write to Maggie with your comments and suggestions for books about your favorite stars at maggiemarron@chickmail.com.

CONTENTS

The picture of paradise: a rocky cliff on the ocean and five delicious babes in white!

Introduction

When *NSYNC's second album, *No Strings Attached*, hit stores, it broke all existing records—including the one set by the Backstreet Boys' *Millennium*! So what is it about this band, made up of a bunch of great friends, who call Orlando their home? Great tunes, great dance moves—and oh yeah, let's not forget just how darn cute each and every one of them is. Yum! Yum! *NSYNC rules!

Welcome to *The Ultimate *NSYNC Quiz Book*. Here's how it works. Each of the quizzes has a bunch of questions for you to answer, which range from the incredibly easy to the truly baffling. The questions are about everything—from what the guys like to eat for breakfast to what their favorite things are to tidbits about the band's history and rise to superstardom. Check your answers and add up your points at the end of each quiz—then move right on to the next one! Don't worry if you don't ace all of the quizzes 'cuz at the end of the book is a bonus quiz where you can pick up even more points before tabulating your final score.

There are side stories throughout this book where you may find an answer or two, but basically you'll have to rely on what you already know! Are you the ultimate *NSYNC fan? It's time to find out just how much you know. Well, don't just stand there—dive in!

Good luck!

Maggie

An early group shot.

iN THE BEGiNNiNG

Beach bums Justin, J.C., Joey, Lance, and Chris pose for a sunset photo.

"When we put the group together we did it ourselves, so we became friends and we started hanging out together, you know, like you would do with your best friend in high school or something, and so when we get time off there won't be a day go by where I don't talk to one of them and say, you know, 'Hey, what are you doing tonight? You wanna go do something?'" —Justin

Who knew that a group of singing friends would ever become such a sensation! Chris, J.C., Justin, Joey, and Lance—that's who! These guys worked their butts off to get where they are because they always believed in themselves, and thank God for that. After all, who could imagine a world without *NSYNC?!? Don't even think about it! Answer these questions to see how much you know about the early years.

1. Whose mom thought up the name *NSYNC?
   a) Justin's
   b) J.C.'s
   c) Lance's
   d) Chris's

2. When was *NSYNC founded?
   a) April of 1995
   b) August of 1995
   c) April of 1996
   d) August of 1996

3. Where did *NSYNC perform their first showcase?
   a) Epcot Center
   b) Universal Studios
   c) Disney World
   d) Seaworld

4. The first single *NSYNC released in the U.S. was:
   a) "Bye, Bye, Bye"
   b) "I Want You Back"
   c) "Tearin' Up My Heart"
   d) "God Must Have Spent a Little More Time On You"

5. Before being signed to a label, the group rehearsed in a large empty warehouse down the road from the house that everyone's moms shared except for:
   a) J.C.'s
   b) Chris'
   c) Justin's
   d) Lance's

6. Where did Justin discover his love for singing?
   a) in church
   b) on the school bus
   c) in the shower
   d) in his school's glee club

*NSYNC stops for a smile as they board their tour bus.

7. *NSYNC got a lucky break when:

    a) 98° canceled their participation in a Disney Channel concert

    b) Backstreet Boys canceled their participation in a Disney Channel concert

    c) Justin talked Jive into giving the guys a chance

    d) Joey and Chris kidnapped a record executive and made him listen to their demo tape

8. *NSYNC's first televised concert aired on:

    a) April 18, 1996

    b) July 16, 1997

    c) July 18, 1998

    d) March 4, 2000

9. Which of the guys got a nickname to make "*NSYNC" match up with their names?

    a) J.C.

    b) Lance

    c) Chris

    d) Joey

10. What year did the guys sign with RCA?

    a) 1995

    b) 1996

    c) 1997

    d) 1998

Answers

1) a; 2) b; 3) c; 4) b; 5) d; 6) a; 7) b; 8) c; 9) b; 10) b

Scoring

Give yourself one point for every right answer.

Total score, quiz #1: _____

*NSYNC 'N concert.

How Well Do You Know...

JOEY?

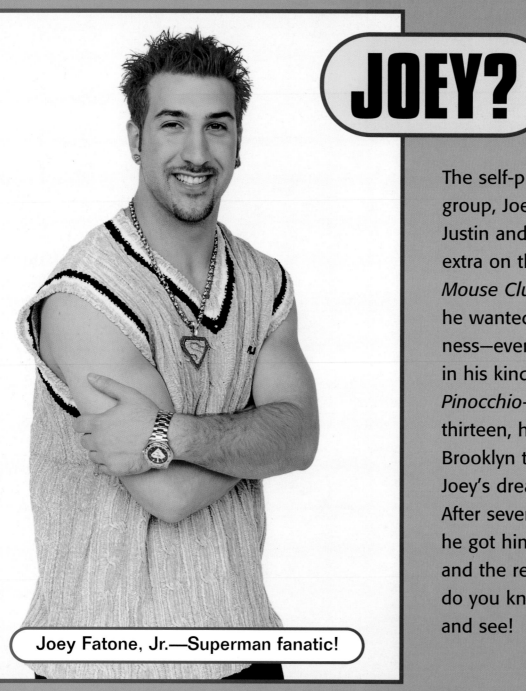

Joey Fatone, Jr.—Superman fanatic!

The self-proclaimed flirt of the group, Joey got "in sync" with Justin and J.C. when he was an extra on the *All-New Mickey Mouse Club.* Joey always knew he wanted to be in show business—even as he played the lead in his kindergarten production of *Pinocchio*—and when he was just thirteen, his family moved from Brooklyn to Orlando to follow Joey's dream of being famous. After several gigs at Disney World, he got himself involved in *MMC*—and the rest is history! How well do you know Joey? Take this quiz and see!

"WE HOPE TO BE SUCCESSFUL, AND WE HOPE WE WILL BE AROUND FOR A LONG TIME." –JOEY

1. How old was Joey when he got his start in show biz?

   a) 7
   b) 11
   c) 13
   d) 15

2. What's Joey's mother's name?

   a) Sandy
   b) Josephine
   c) Lana
   d) Phyllis

3. Joey's favorite cartoon character is:

   a) Batman
   b) Superman
   c) Squirtle
   d) Popeye

4. What's Joey's favorite Adam Sandler movie?

   a) Billy Madison
   b) Big Daddy
   c) Airheads
   d) The Wedding Singer

5. Joey's favorite actor is:

   a) Al Pacino
   b) Robert DeNiro
   c) Adam Sandler
   d) Jim Belushi

6. Joey's favorite movie actress is:

   a) Susan Sarandon
   b) Annette Bening
   c) Jodie Foster
   d) Michelle Pfeiffer

7. Who is Joey's dream woman?

   a) Julia Roberts
   b) Rebecca Romijn-Stamos
   c) Brandy
   d) Demi Moore

8. Joey's favorite song is:

   a) "The Right Stuff" by New Kids on the Block
   b) "Water Runs Dry" by Boyz II Men
   c) "The Thong Song" by Sisqo
   d) "Girls on Film" by Duran Duran

9. Who's Joey's favorite Spice Girl?

   a) Baby Spice
   b) Sporty Spice
   c) Ginger Spice
   d) Scary Spice

10. Joey's favorite author is:

   a) Tom Clancy
   b) Helen Fielding
   c) William Shakespeare
   d) Herman Melville

11. Joey's favorite kind of food is:

   a) Japanese
   b) Mexican
   c) French
   d) Italian

12. What's Joey's favorite bevvie?

   a) Pepsi
   b) Coke
   c) Mountain Dew
   d) 7 Up

13. What's Joey's favorite holiday?

   a) Valentine's Day
   b) Columbus Day
   c) Thanksgiving
   d) Christmas

14. What's Joey's favorite animal?

   a) tiger
   b) lion
   c) panther
   d) cow

15. Which of these is one of Joey's nicknames?

   a) Phat-One
   b) Jo-ah-le-le
   c) Mr. Cool Hair
   d) none of the above

16. Joey's worst habit is:

   a) picking his toenails
   b) chewing his tongue
   c) burping in public
   d) biting his fingernails

17. What's Joey's favorite city?

   a) New York
   b) Paris
   c) New Orleans
   d) London

 15

18. What's Joey's hobby?

a) going to the movies
b) video games
c) jet skiing
d) all of the above

19. What was the name of the group Joey's father, Joseph Fatone, Sr., used to belong to?

a) the Bunions
b) the Horizons
c) the Orions
d) the Big Dippers

20. What styles of dance has Joey studied?

a) jazz
b) ballet
c) tap
d) all of the above

21. What's the name of the girl with whom Joey shared his first kiss?

a) Lanni
b) Lisa
c) Lily
d) Laura

22. What's Joey's favorite movie?

a) <u>The Shining</u>
b) <u>The Sound of Music</u>
c) <u>Willie Wonka and the Chocolate Factory</u>
d) <u>West Side Story</u>

23. Joey's most embarrassing moment was when he:

a) tripped over his shoelace at a press conference
b) had a big zit on his nose during a photo shoot
c) appeared on stage with his fly unzipped
d) forgot his mother's first name

24. If Joey had one wish granted to him, it would be:

a) more money
b) more friends
c) more wishes
d) none of the above

25. Joey's middle name is:

a) Alan
b) Antoine
c) Anthony
d) Andrew

Scoring

Give yourself one point for every right answer.

Total score, quiz #2: _____

Answers:

1) c; 2) d; 3) b; 4) a; 5) b; 6) c; 7) d; 8) b; 9) c; 10) c; 11) d; 12) a; 13) d; 14) c; 15) a; 16) c; 17) d; 18) d; 19) c; 20) d; 21) b; 22) c; 23) c; 24) c; 25) c

Joey poses with a feline friend.

*NSYNC all decked out and on the town.

*NSYNC: Fact or Fiction—Part 1

J.C. and Lance at Planet Hollywood.

There are a lot of rumors floating around about the guys from *NSYNC. And also a lot of just plain wrong information. Can you separate the fact from the fiction? Take this quiz and see!

1. Justin hails from Nashville, Tennessee.

2. The title of the group's second album is Just Got Paid.

3. The guys consider the band's hometown to be Orlando.

4. Chris was the last member to join the band.

5. Joey is the self-proclaimed shyest member of the band.

6. "It's hard to say I'm sorry,...It's hard to make the things I did undone" is a line from the song "I Drive Myself Crazy."

7. Justin and Joey were castmates on the Mickey Mouse Club.

8. The group's first smash hit was "Tearin' Up My Heart."

9. Boyz II Men is one of the group's biggest musical influences.

10. Justin's sign is Capricorn.

11. J.C. is the oldest member of *NSYNC.

12. Lance's dream car is a Porsche 944.

13. J.C.'s favorite NFL team is the Washington Redskins.

14. Chris is the only brown-eyed guy in the group.

15. Before being released in the U.S., *NSYNC's debut album was released in Germany.

16. Joey is a huge Superman fan.

17. The other guys in the band call J.C. "Big Daddy."

18. J.C.'s favorite holiday is Halloween.

19. The other band members refer to Lance as Lansten and Bass.

20. *NSYNC recorded a single with Gloria Estefan for the soundtrack to the movie Face the Music starring Marisa Tomei.

21. Chris came up with the idea for the war setting in the video for "God Must Have Spent a Little More Time On You."

22. When he's not working or sleeping, J.C. likes to watch movies.

23. The original *NSYNC trio met Joey in a club.

24. Before joining *NSYNC, J.C. had small roles in movies and on the TV show SeaQuest.

25. Chris's favorite food is tacos.

26. J.C.'s birthday is August 6, 1976.

27. Lance is the tallest member of *NSYNC.

28. Lance makes sure the other guys eat and get enough rest.

29. Justin's first date took place at the movies.

30. Chris grew up in Orlando, Florida.

Dive in—the water's H-O-T!

Answers

Scoring

Give yourself one point for every right answer.

Total score, quiz #3: _____

⊗NSYNC:
Secrets for Success

"As far as image, we're just five guys doing the music that we like to do. We don't pay too much attention to this boy band phenomenon. We just enjoy what we do and being on top and having fun. We consider ourselves a vocal group, because that's what we started off to do. We just want to entertain." **—Justin**

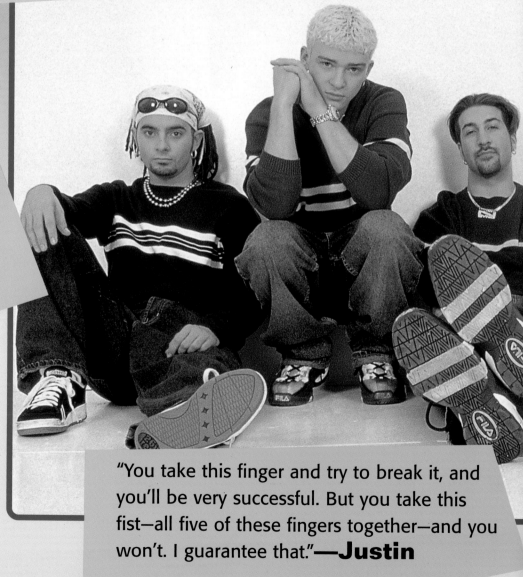

"You can be nobody one day, and a big star the next day, and a nobody the day after that." **—Chris**

"You take this finger and try to break it, and you'll be very successful. But you take this fist—all five of these fingers together—and you won't. I guarantee that." **—Justin**

No matter how talented you are, you will never be successful if you don't focus and work really hard. No one knows that better than the *NSYNC guys! And once you get to the top, you have to respect the people who helped you get there. Otherwise, you can enjoy your 15 minutes of fame and then good-bye, Gus! Here's what the guys have to say about getting—and staying—famous.

"Just follow your dreams, like we did. I mean, we've always dreamed of it, and never given up on that dream." —**Lance**

"Have respect for everyone." —**J.C.**

"We know that there's a million other groups doing this, but we want to be one of the few that are around for a long time. And we feel the only way to do that is be ourselves, because people will see through an act, and people will see through the phoniness. But if they see something genuine, and they see something real, then we should have no problem." —**J.C.**

"Always try your best and if there's a weak spot, try to work on it as hard as you can. Put all your effort and focus into it." —**Joey**

*NSYNC has what it takes to succeed—talent, drive, and utter cuteness!

25

A phony movie poster plugging the guys.

And the award goes to… *NSYNC at the 72nd Annual Academy Awards.

How Well Do You Know...

JUSTIN?

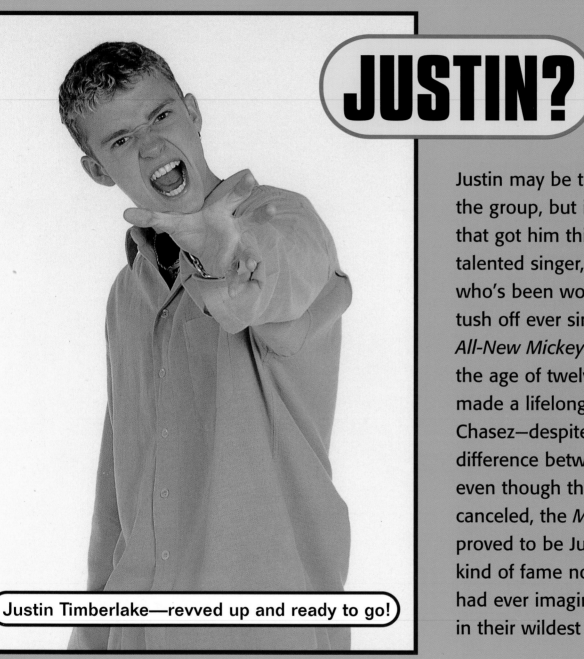

Justin Timberlake—revved up and ready to go!

Justin may be the little darling in the group, but it isn't mere looks that got him this far. Justin is a talented singer, dancer, and actor who's been working his cute little tush off ever since he joined *The All-New Mickey Mouse Club* at the age of twelve. There, he made a lifelong friend in J.C. Chasez—despite the five-year age difference between them. And even though the show was soon canceled, the *MMC* connection proved to be Justin's ticket to the kind of fame none of the guys had ever imagined possible—even in their wildest dreams!

"MY LIFE IS LIKE A FAIRY TALE. EVERY DAY I RECEIVE ABOUT 500 FAN LETTERS. IT FEELS GREAT TO BE LIKED." —JUSTIN

1. **What's Justin's middle name?**
   a) Richard
   b) Randall
   c) Robert
   d) Ripley

2. **When did Justin join the MMC cast?**
   a) 1990
   b) 1991
   c) 1992
   d) 1993

3. **What was the first group Justin ever saw in concert?**
   a) The Beach Boys
   b) The B-52s
   c) The Thompson Twins
   d) Boyz II Men

4. **How old was Justin when he moved to Orlando?**
   a) 3
   b) 5
   c) 7
   d) 9

5. **What's Justin's mother's name?**
   a) Shelly
   b) Lynn
   c) Denise
   d) Alannah

6. **Who is Justin's favorite model?**
   a) Kate Moss
   b) Tyra Banks
   c) Linda Evangelista
   d) Iman

7. **Who's Justin's dream girl?**
   a) Mandy Moore
   b) Jessica Simpson
   c) Jennifer Aniston
   d) Katie Couric

8. **Who is Justin's favorite author?**
   a) Stephen King
   b) John Grisham
   c) Mary Higgins Clark
   d) Carl Hiaasen

9. **What's Justin's favorite sport to play?**
   a) football
   b) lacrosse
   c) basketball
   d) baseball

10. **Who are Justin's favorite actresses?**
    a) Sandra Bullock and Meg Ryan
    b) Demi Moore and Michelle Pfeiffer
    c) Julia Roberts and Winona Ryder
    d) Gilda Radner and Goldie Hawn

11. **What's Justin's favorite holiday?**
    a) Christmas
    b) Independence Day
    c) Thanksgiving
    d) Halloween

12. **Who's Justin's favorite athlete?**
    a) Tiger Woods
    b) Michael Jordan
    c) Patrick Ewing
    d) Mia Hamm

13. **Justin's favorite animals are:**
    a) turtles
    b) elephants
    c) alligators
    d) dogs

14. **Where does Justin love to vacation most?**
    a) Europe
    b) Vermont
    c) Hawaii
    d) Disney World

15. **Justin really hates:**
    a) snakes
    b) his curly hair
    c) smoking
    d) all of the above

16. **Justin's cat's name is:**
    a) Aleshia
    b) Alley
    c) Allison
    d) Alex

17. **What are Justin's favorite cereals?**
    a) Grape-Nuts and Mueslix
    b) Apple Jacks and Cap'n Crunch
    c) Total and Corn Flakes
    d) Cinnamon Toast Crunch and Frosted Mini Wheats

Justin hangs out in his casual duds.

18. Justin's favorite food is:

a) pasta
b) pizza
c) peanut butter
d) pickles

19. Which of these is not one of Justin's nicknames?

a) Curly
b) Mr. Smooth
c) Justice
d) Bounce

20. What's Justin's favorite color?

a) orange
b) baby blue
c) pink
d) beige

21. Which of the following does Justin consider a musical influence?

a) Peter Gabriel
b) Jimi Hendrix
c) Alice Cooper
d) all of the above

22. Justin's favorite TV show is:

a) Popular
b) Dawson's Creek
c) Frasier
d) Friends

23. Justin's favorite horror film/thriller is:

a) A Nightmare on Elm Street
b) The Sixth Sense
c) Scream
d) Halloween

24. Which of these is one of Justin's favorite movies?

a) The Usual Suspects
b) Hudson Hawk
c) It Happened One Night
d) Annie Hall

25. Who's Justin's favorite actor?

a) Brad Pitt
b) Tommy Lee Jones
c) Jim Carrey
d) all of the above

Hey Justin—ever hear of a little thing called a bathing suit?!?

Scoring

Give yourself one point for every right answer.

Total score, quiz #4: _____

Answers:

1) b; 2) d; 3) a; 4) c; 5) b; 6) b; 7) c; 8) b; 9) c; 10) b; 11) a; 12) b;
13) d; 14) c; 15) d; 16) b; 17) b; 18) a; 19) c; 20) b; 21) d; 22) b; 23) c;
24) a; 25) d

Who the Heck Is That?!? — Part I

Could you pick your fave *NSYNC-er out of a crowd? Would you know him just by hearing one little fact about him? Try this quiz and find out!

1. He once played a character called Clarence "Wipeout" Adams.

2. He won a local contest, "Dance Like New Kids on the Block."

3. He's originally from Brooklyn, New York.

4. He counts the Beatles as a musical influence.

5. He once worked as a vocal coach.

6. He's considered the "Daddy" of the group.

7. He once belonged to a competition choir called Attache.

8. He once considered working for NASA and even passed the NASA entrance exam.

9. He thinks his arms and chest are too skinny.

10. He once broke his thumb while performing.

11. He has a Superman tattoo on his ankle.

12. His nicknames are Lucky and Crazy.

13. He's the oldest member of *NSYNC.

14. He has a dog named Ozzie.

15. He played the lead role in his kindergarten production of *Pinocchio.*

16. Francy was the name of his first love.

17. He can't stand that none of the other guys listen to him when he speaks.

18. He especially likes people who aren't afraid to speak their mind.

19. He collects sneakers.

20. His favorite holiday is Halloween.

21. He admits that he can be very stubborn.

22. He always forgets his stuff in hotel rooms.

23. His worst habits are burping and constantly clearing his throat.

24. He was the final addition to the group.

25. He played a small part in *Once Upon a Time in America,* which starred Robert DeNiro.

Scoring

Give yourself one point for every right answer.

Total score, quiz #5: _____

The guys show off their Blockbuster Entertainment award.

Answers:

1. J.C.; 2. Justin; 3. Joey; 4. Chris; 5. Lance; 6. J.C.; 7. Lance; 8. Lance; 9. J.C.; 10. Justin; 11. Joey; 12. Chris; 13. Chris; 14. Justin; 15. Joey; 16. Joey; 17. Lance; 18. Joey; 19. Justin; 20. Chris; 21. J.C.; 22. Chris; 23. Justin; 24. Lance; 25. Joey

Bye, Bye, Bye!

THE MUSIC

"There's nothing better than going out with your friends and having a good time, and that's what it is. These guys are my best friends and when we get to go out we get to see each other have fun. And that's like the best part about the job."
—J.C.

That—and, of course, making music, which is what these guys were born to do. Someday, they'd like to do all their own original songs—in fact, J.C. helped write two songs on *No Strings Attached*—but they're so busy singing and performing that there just isn't any time. Maybe on the next album! In the meantime, take this quiz and see how much you know about *NSYNC's music.

The *NSYNC totem pole.

The guys get down with one of their musicians.

1. Lisa "Left Eye" Lopes is featured on what *NSYNC song?

   a) "Just Got Paid"
   b) "Digital Get Down"
   c) "Space Cowboy"
   d) "I Thought She Knew"

2. Their favorite song to perform in concert is:

   a) "Here We Go"
   b) "God Must Have Spent a Little More Time On You"
   c) "Tearin' Up My Heart"
   d) "I Want You Back"

3. Before every concert the guys do this for luck:

   a) play a game of hackey sack
   b) pray
   c) give each other high-fives
   d) call their mothers

4. *NSYNC's first single, "I Want You Back," was released in the United States in:

   a) February of 1998
   b) December of 1998
   c) February of 1997
   d) December of 1997

5. When did their first album go double platinum?

   a) June 1997
   b) September 1997
   c) May 1998
   d) September 1998

6. Which group most inspires *NSYNC?

   a) New Kids on the Block
   b) Boyz II Men
   c) The Backstreet Boys
   d) The Jackson 5

7. What is the title of their Christmas CD?

   a) <u>Santa and Me</u>
   b) <u>Home for Christmas</u>
   c) <u>A Very Special *NSYNC Christmas</u>
   d) <u>Christmas Sounds</u>

8. J.C. co-penned and co-produced "Space Cowboy" and this song from <u>No Strings Attached</u>:

   a) "Bye, Bye, Bye"
   b) "It's Gonna Be Me"
   c) "Digital Get Down"
   d) "I Thought She Knew"

9. This group recorded a version of "God Must Have Spent a Little More Time On You" with the *NSYNC guys singing backing vocals:

   a) The BeeGees
   b) Alabama
   c) 98°
   d) Santana

10. How long did it take the guys to make the video for "Bye, Bye, Bye"?

   a) 4 weeks
   b) 4 days
   c) 4 hours
   d) none of the above

ANSWERS

1) c; 2) b; 3) a; 4) a; 5) d; 6) b; 7) b; 8) c; 9) b; 10) b

SCORING

Give yourself one point for every right answer.

Total score, quiz #6: _____

"We're number one!"

What I Hate About Me...
The Guys Tell All!

Sure, we all have things we just hate about ourselves—but could the perfect *NSYNC babes be less than satisfied with themselves? Believe it or not, it's absolutely true! All of the guys have flaws they wish they could change.

JUSTIN

For instance, Justin admits that he cannot pass a mirror without checking himself out. Now, it's not because he's in love with himself or anything. Oh no. It's to make sure his hair isn't freaking out. Now even though most of us adore Justin's curly locks, he can't stand them. He always feels like his hair is out of control and when he passes a mirror, he just can't resist the urge to check on that unruly mop!

The other thing Justin would like to change about himself is that he's a huge procrastinator. Yep, he's one of those "never do today what you can put off till tomorrow" types. Well, I guess it's one thing if you have a history paper to hand in or a bedroom to clean—even a book deadline—but I guess if you're going to continue to be a superstar, procrastinating is something you really need to work on!

JOEY

And what about Joey? Well, you'll never catch him being a phony as this is the kind of person he hates the most—but what does he dislike about himself? Number one, without question, has to be his feet. He thinks they're too big and says, "I step on people's feet everywhere I go!" He also dislikes his nose, and although he's never really said why, it's probably because at night, when everyone's trying to sleep, it becomes his own personal trumpet. Yes, Joey is a first-class snorer—and he wishes he could stop snoring because all of his bandmates tease him about it!

CHRIS

Like Joey, Chris dislikes his feet—but because he thinks they're too small! Well, he can't change that unless he walks around in Sideshow Bob shoes— but there are a couple of things he doesn't like about himself that he knows he could work on. Like his nails. Chris bites these practically down to the bone and he hates the way this makes his hands look. Also, he has a really short attention span—probably because he's forever planning *NSYNC's next step—which he'd like to improve.

LANCE

Like Justin, Lance dislikes his hair because he can't control it. It is hard to style, he has confessed, because it's just too thick. Like everyone else in the band, he also bites his nails, and like Chris, he hates looking at his hands because of it! Lance also hates the fact that he's so messy.

J.C.

J.C. seems pretty happy about himself, actually—or maybe this writer hasn't heard of any of his flaws!! He does think his arms and chest are too skinny. Well, that's easily changed in three words, silly boy: work that bod!

How Well Do You Know...

CHRIS?

"I'M THE TROUBLE.
I'M THE POISON
IN THE GROUP."
–CHRIS

Oh Chris, let's not go that far! Sure, he is the resident bad boy—and joker—but without Chris, there might not have been an *NSYNC. It was Chris who got tired of waiting for his big break, and when he met Joey, J.C., and Justin and started hanging out with them, he knew they could be the next big thing. How much do you know about Chris? Take this quiz and find out!

Chris Kirkpatrick—aspiring psychologist?

1. **What's Chris's middle name?**
   a) Alex
   b) Alan
   c) Anton
   d) Adam

2. **What's Chris's Zodiac sign?**
   a) Aries
   b) Cancer
   c) Libra
   d) Scorpio

3. **Where was Chris born?**
   a) Clarion, Pennsylvania
   b) Wexville, Pennsylvania
   c) Pittsburgh, Pennsylvania
   d) Hamburg, Pennsylvania

4. **What's Chris's mother's name?**
   a) Barbara
   b) Beverly
   c) Bonnie
   d) Billy Sue

5. **What does Chris collect?**
   a) baseball cards
   b) action figures
   c) records
   d) video games

6. **Which of these is Chris's favorite movie?**
   a) Indiana Jones and the Temple of Doom
   b) Moonstruck
   c) Mad Max
   d) Kiss the Girls

7. **Which of these is Chris's favorite actress?**
   a) Audrey Hepburn
   b) Meryl Streep
   c) Meg Ryan
   d) Goldie Hawn

8. **Chris's dream girl is:**
   a) Gloria Estefan
   b) Gwen Stefani
   c) Britney Spears
   d) Neve Campbell

9. **Chris's beverage of choice is:**
   a) chocolate milk
   b) Sprite
   c) tomato juice
   d) orange juice

10. **Chris's favorite animals are:**
    a) monkeys
    b) tigers
    c) giraffes
    d) cats

11. **Chris's hobby is:**
    a) collecting stamps
    b) writing songs
    c) collecting matchbooks
    d) all of the above

12. **What sport does Chris like to play?**
    a) basketball
    b) football
    c) roller hockey
    d) all of the above

13. **What is Chris's worst habit?**
    a) smoking
    b) picking his toes
    c) biting his fingernails
    d) swearing

14. **Chris's favorite childhood memory is:**
    a) going to his grandma's house
    b) playing with his dog
    c) mowing the lawn
    d) going to camp

15. **Chris's favorite vacation spot is:**
    a) Montego Bay, Jamaica
    b) Cancún, Mexico
    c) Honolulu, Hawaii
    d) Paris, France

16. **Chris says that he smiles all the time now that he:**
    a) has a girlfriend
    b) got his braces off
    c) is rich and famous
    d) all of the above

17. **What's the first album Chris ever bought?**
    a) Rio by Duran Duran
    b) Thriller by Michael Jackson
    c) Like a Virgin by Madonna
    d) Synchronicity by the Police

20. Who are Chris's favorite singers?

a) Michael Jackson and Brian McKnight
b) Brian Littrell and A.J. McLean
c) Stevie Wonder and Neil Young
d) Madonna and Mariah Carey

21. Who's Chris's fave Spice Girl?

a) Baby Spice
b) Scary Spice
c) Baby Spice
d) Posh Spice

22. Who are Chris's favorite singing groups?

a) Matchbox 20 and TLC
b) New Kids on the Block and O-Town
c) Green Day and No Doubt
d) Genesis and the Doors

23. What's Chris's favorite kind of food?

a) Mexican
b) Chinese
c) French
d) Italian

24. What are Chris's favorite colors?

a) fuchsia and tangerine
b) black and silver
c) purple and yellow
d) blue and red

25. Which of the following was one of Chris's former jobs?

a) lifeguard
b) movie theater usher
c) DJ
d) security guard

"When I grow up, I want to be this famous!"

18. When Chris was growing up, he thought he'd be:

a) a singer
b) a veterinarian
c) an actor
d) a psychologist

19. How tall is Chris?

a) 5'6"
b) 5'9"
c) 5'11"
d) over 6' tall!

Answers:

24) b; 25) c

1) b; 2) c; 3) a; 4) b; 5) c; 6) c; 7) a; 8) b; 9) d; 10) b; 11) b; 12) d;
13) c; 14) a; 15) b; 16) b; 17) b; 18) c; 19) c; 20) a; 21) d; 22) d; 23) a;

Scoring

Give yourself one point for every right answer.

Total score, quiz #1: _____

44

Chris—pre mop-top chop.

*NSYNC: Fact or Fiction—Part II

More truth, more lies. Can you tell which? Take the next part of this quiz and find out!

1. J.C.'s worst habit is that he picks his nose.
2. Lance is the youngest member of *NSYNC.
3. Justin's most prized possession is his voice.
4. Joey is a native of Orlando.
5. Chris has an "innie."
6. Justin took tuba lessons when he was younger.
7. Joey performed in Universal Studios' Beetlejuice Graveyard Revue, as Beetlejuice.
8. J.C. loves Harry Connick, Jr. and Billie Holiday.
9. Chris says that he is a suit and tie type of guy.
10. Justin has lots of sisters.
11. J.C.'s favorite snack is potato chips.
12. Joey loves to play all sports.
13. Sometimes Chris is really lazy and it annoys his bandmates.
14. Lance left his family behind when he moved to Orlando to join *NSYNC.
15. Joey was named after his mother, Josephine, who is known to friends and family as "Joey."
16. Justin's favorite singer is himself.
17. Chris dislikes techno music because he thinks it's too loud and harsh.
18. Lance is the least interested in the financial side of the music industry.
19. In the band's early years, management encouraged Joey to grow a goatee and pierce his eyebrow so he could be the "bad boy."
20. J.C. had been singing professionally for years before auditioning for MMC.
21. Lance is totally hyper all the time.
22. Joey is older than J.C.
23. Justin created *NSYNC.
24. Chris has two earring holes in each ear.
25. J.C.'s fairly thick-skinned and usually takes criticism pretty well.
26. J.C. has an "outie."
27. Justin loves chocolate chip ice cream.
28. Lance never thought he would be able to make a living as a performer.
29. Joey is a boxers kind of guy.
30. Chris's favorite word is "dude."

Is Lance good enough for the kickline?

Answers

1. Fiction. Thank God, fiction, it's that he sleeps too much! 2. Fiction—it's Justin! 3. Fact 4. Fiction. Joey's family moved to Orlando when Joey was 13. 5. Fact 6. Fiction. But he did take both piano and guitar lessons. 7. Fiction. While he did perform in this revue, he played Dracula and the Wolfman, not Beetlejuice. 8. Fact 9. Fiction. Chris is definitely a jeans and T-shirt type of guy. 10. Fiction. He actually has two half-brothers: Jonathan and Steven. 11. Fiction. It's ice cream—especially mint chocolate chip or chocolate chip cookie dough! 12. Fiction. While Joey enjoys activities like in-line skating and jet skiing, he's not a sports fan. 13. As Fiction as can be. In fact, Justin says that Chris's energy has been a real asset to the group. 14. Fiction. They all moved to Orlando with him, but when he turned 18, he found his own apartment and his family moved back home. 15. Fiction. He's named after his dad, Joe. His mom's name is Phyllis! 16. Fiction. While he likes his voice, he's a really big fan of Notorious B.I.G. and Stevie Wonder. 17. Fiction. Chris loves dancing to techno music. 18. Fiction. He's the most interested of all the guys. In fact, the other members of the group have said that Lance is always coming up with new ideas for merchandise or spin-off projects. 19. Fiction. Joey walked into the band with his goatee and pierced eyebrow and fought to keep them! 20. Fiction. Before he auditioned for MMC, the only singing J.C. had done was in the shower! 21. Fiction. Lance is actually a very laid-back dude. 22. Fiction. J.C. was born in 1976, but Joey was born in 1977. 23. Fiction. It was Chris who started the group because he got sick of waiting for his big break to happen. He decided to make it happen and put the group together. 24. Fact 25. Fiction. Criticism makes J.C. feel pretty insecure—but he tries to ignore it. 26. Fiction. He's an inie! 27. Fact 28. Fact 29. Fiction. He's most comfortable in briefs, by Fruit of the Loom. 30. Fact

Scoring

Give yourself one point for every right answer.

Total score, quiz #8: _____

47

BEHIND THE SCENES

"Everything we do is always together and I think that's what makes our group unique." —Lance

The *NSYNC guys try out their sea legs.

48

How well do you know the guys behind the curtain—the real facts about their lives together, and before they were *NSYNC? Take this quiz to test your general knowledge of the guys!

1. What's a habit all the members of *NSYNC share?

   a) they all smoke
   b) they all tap their feet
   c) they all bite their nails
   d) they all pick their noses

2. Which two members of *NSYNC attended the same high school?

   a) J.C. and Joey
   b) J.C. and Lance
   c) Justin and Chris
   d) Lance and Joey

3. Which member of *NSYNC drives a black Jeep Cherokee?

   a) Chris
   b) Joey
   c) Lance
   d) J.C.

4. Who worked with the same vocal coach as Justin?

   a) Chris
   b) J.C.
   c) Lance
   d) Joey

5. Which member of *NSYNC had a puppy he had to give away because of his busy schedule?

   a) Joey
   b) J.C.
   c) Lance
   d) Justin

6. Who's the group's resident surfer?

   a) Lance
   b) Chris
   c) J.C.
   d) Justin

7. Which *NSYNC-er really hates dressing up?

   a) J.C.
   b) Lance
   c) Chris
   d) all of the above

The guys sleep in bunk beds on the tour bus.

*NSYNC singing around an open fire.

8. Which member of *NSYNC appears on <u>People</u>'s list of <u>America's 100 Most Eligible Bachelors</u>?

   a) Justin
   b) Lance
   c) J.C.
   d) all of the above

9. The rest of the guys describe which member as a real businessman?

   a) J.C.
   b) Justin
   c) Lance
   d) Joey

10. Which guy always brings a video camera with him while they're on the road?

   a) J.C.
   b) Joey
   c) Lance
   d) Chris

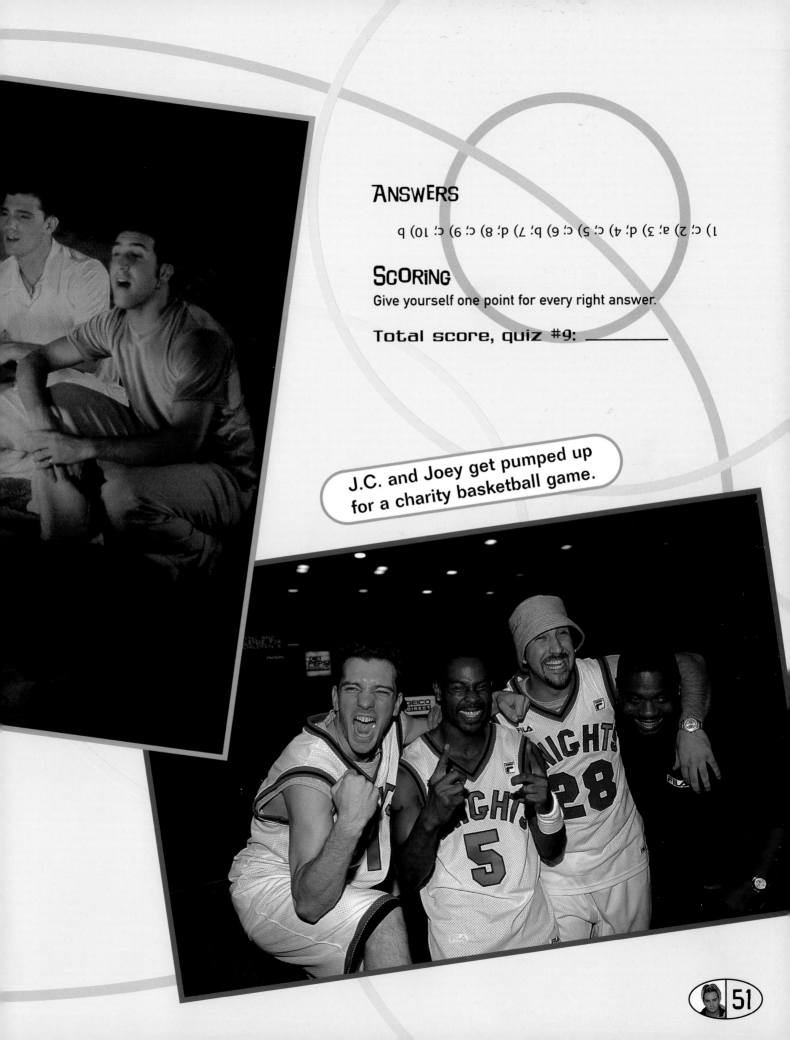

ANSWERS

1) c; 2) a; 3) d; 4) c; 5) c; 6) b; 7) d; 8) p; 9) c; 10) b

SCORING

Give yourself one point for every right answer.

Total score, quiz #9: _____

J.C. and Joey get pumped up for a charity basketball game.

It's in the Stars

Are you a perfect love match with your favorite guy? Read on and find out!

J.C. Chasez, Leo

Characteristics of Leos:

- romantic
- affectionate
- loyal
- talented leaders
- love to be the center of attention
- sympathetic to others
- honest in all of their endeavors
- intellectual
- warmhearted
- generous

Perfect matches for Leos:

- Aries
- Gemini
- Sagittarius
- Libra

Bad matches for Leos:

- Taurus
- Scorpio

Chris Kirkpatrick, Libra

Characteristics of Libras:

- sensitive
- charming
- able to succeed in both business and social life
- tactful
- sensitive
- well-liked
- admired for their remarkable sense of justice
- good managers and teachers

Perfect matches for Libras:

- Leo
- Gemini
- Sagittarius
- Aquarius

Bad matches for Libras:

- Cancer
- Capricorn

Characteristics of Aquarians:

- sincere
- warmhearted
- able to ease the tension in any situation
- diplomatic
- clear in their own demands, but not stubborn enough to ignore the value of compromise
- keen-minded
- endlessly creative
- natural-born leaders
- natural entertainers
- loyal
- loving
- usually marry for life

Perfect matches for Aquarians:

- Aries
- Gemini
- Libra
- Sagittarius

Bad matches for Aquarians:

- Taurus
- Scorpio

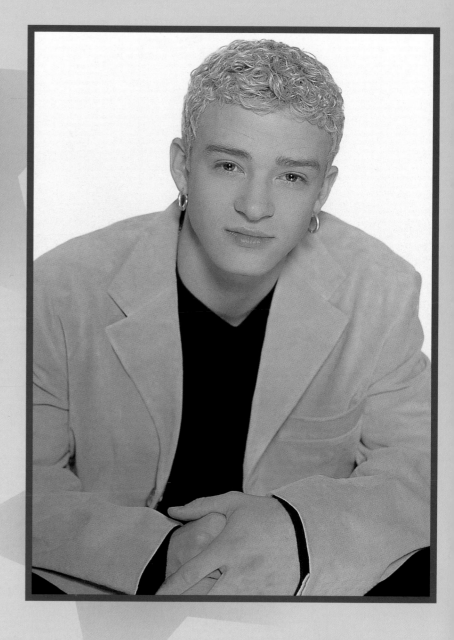

Characteristics of Taureans:

- slow and methodical
- practical and reserved
- tenacious and determined
- possessing tremendous willpower and self-discipline
- generally easygoing, slow to anger, but fierce-tempered once aroused
- loyal
- warm
- loving
- gentle
- charming
- cautious
- good at business
- artistic
- thorough

Perfect matches for Taureans:

- Cancer
- Virgo
- Capricorn
- Pisces

Bad matches for Taureans:

- Leo
- Aquarius

*NSYNC stop to smell the flowers.

57

Riding horseback—bareback!—down the beach.

How Well Do You Know...

LANCE?

Lance was the last member to join the group. In fact, he may never have met up with the other guys if he didn't have the same vocal coach as Justin. You see, there was already a fifth member of the band, but he wasn't dedicated enough so they had to let him go. Justin asked his vocal coach if he knew any good bass singers—and the band found its bass—in a Bass! What do you know about Lance? Take this quiz to see if you know as much as you think you do.

Lance Bass—He's got it goin' on all right!

"WE LOVE OUR FANS. OUR FANS ARE WHAT MAKES US. WE LOVE SPENDING TIME WITH THEM AND MEETING EVERYBODY. OUR FANS ARE JUST INCREDIBLE." —LANCE

1. **Lance's first name is actually:**
   a) Lansten
   b) James
   c) Joseph
   d) Jerome

2. **Lance joined his school chorus in what grade?**
   a) sixth
   b) seventh
   c) eighth
   d) ninth

3. **Lance was in a statewide chorus called:**
   a) Mississippi Show Tunes
   b) Mississippi Show Chorus
   c) Mississippi Show Stoppers
   d) Mississippi Show Time

4. **Which of the following is not one of Lance's nicknames:**
   a) Lansten
   b) Big Daddy
   c) Scoop
   d) Mr. Cool

5. **Lance's Zodiac sign is:**
   a) Sagittarius
   b) Leo
   c) Cancer
   d) Taurus

6. **Lance has a sister named:**
   a) Stephanie
   b) Stacy
   c) Susan
   d) Shelly

7. **Lance collects:**
   a) Tazmanian Devil memorabilia
   b) stamps
   c) old comic books
   d) all of the above

8. **Lance's first job was dressing up like:**
   a) Tony the Tiger
   b) Barney
   c) a big dog named Poofoo
   d) a clown named Bobo

9. **Lance's favorite actor is:**
   a) Tom Hanks
   b) Mel Gibson
   c) Burt Reynolds
   d) Matthew Perry

10. **One of Lance's favorite actresses is:**
    a) Demi Moore
    b) Jennifer Aniston
    c) Julia Roberts
    d) Salma Hayek

11. **Lance's favorite breakfast food is:**
    a) pancakes
    b) Belgian waffles
    c) French toast
    d) scrambled eggs

12. **Lance exclaimed, "I fell in love fifty-one times today!" while at:**
    a) the mall signing autographs
    b) the Miss America Pageant
    c) the Miss Teen USA Pageant
    d) a night club

13. **Lance's favorite getaway is:**
    a) Disney World
    b) the beach
    c) the arcade
    d) his parents' house

14. **Lance's most embarrassing moment was at a party when he did an impression of:**
    a) an airplane taking off
    b) a hen laying an egg
    c) a dog burying a bone
    d) a squirrel eating a nut

15. **If Lance could change one thing about himself it would be:**
    a) his nose
    b) to be taller
    c) to have blue eyes
    d) his ears

16. **What does Lance drive?**
    a) a black Toyota 4Runner
    b) a white Corvette
    c) a blue Mustang convertible
    d) a green pickup truck

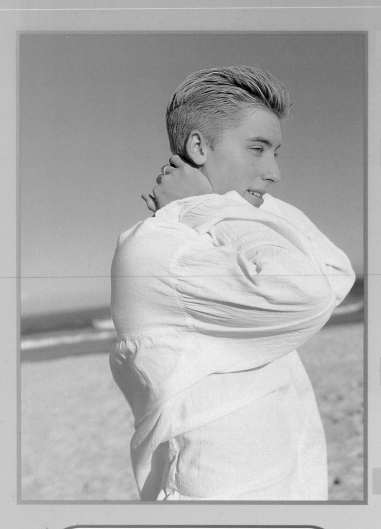

Lance takes a moment to reflect on his life on the beach—one of his fave places to be.

20. On which TV show did Lance have a guest appearance?

a) Buffy the Vampire Slayer
b) Seventh Heaven
c) Ally McBeal
d) Will and Grace

21. What's his favorite current TV show?

a) Friends
b) NYPD Blue
c) Survivor
d) Third Rock From the Sun

22. What's Lance's favorite movie?

a) Fried Green Tomatoes
b) Mortal Kombat Annihilation
c) End of Days
d) Casablanca

23. What's Lance's favorite color?

a) baby blue
b) lavender
c) candy apple red
d) bright yellow

24. Which of these is Lance's favorite group?

a) the Offspring
b) Green Day
c) Nine Days
d) Matchbox 20

25. Who is Lance's favorite singer?

a) John Secada
b) Garth Brooks
c) Vince Gill
d) Randy Travis

17. What's Lance's fave beverage?

a) apple juice
b) Dr. Pepper
c) prune juice
d) Sprite

18. Which is Lance's favorite team sport?

a) hockey
b) basketball
c) volleyball
d) baseball

19. What's Lance's fave type of food?

a) Mexican
b) Japanese
c) Chinese
d) Italian

Answers:

1) b; 2) b; 3) c; 4) b; 5) d; 6) b; 7) d; 8) c; 9) a; 10) b; 11) c; 12) c;
13) b; 14) d; 15) b; 16) a; 17) b; 18) c; 19) a; 20) b; 21) d; 22) d; 23) b; 24) a; 25) b

Scoring

Give yourself one point for every right answer.

Total score, quiz #10: _____

62

Lance looking adorable in overalls.

*NSYNC posing with fans.

I wonder whose birthday it is?

Fans line up outside MTV Studios in Times Square, New York City, to get a glimpse of their fave guys.

Who the Heck Is That?!? — Part II

Back for more, are ya? Okay, here are some more random facts. See if you can match up the fact to the right guy!

1. He's the group "cheerleader."
2. His parents' names are Jim and Diane.
3. He sleeps in Calvin Klein pajamas.
4. He especially dislikes moody people.
5. He says his mom is the strongest person he knows.
6. He says that he took his life in his hands when he surfed in a hurricane.
7. His mother's name is Karen.
8. He loves to use the word "crunk," which means crazy or cool.
9. He's the most likely to look after the other guys.
10. His birthday is May 4, 1979.
11. He really enjoys horseback riding.
12. He had a small role on the TV show *SeaQuest*.
13. His most embarrassing onstage moment was when he only got halfway over in a flip and landed on his face.

14. He spends the most time on his hair.
15. He does not like to be teased about his snoring.
16. He loves animals and plans to buy a ranch with a few horses in the future.
17. He says that he has a really short attention span.
18. He's the group's biggest flirt.
19. He thinks his feet are too small.
20. His favorite article of clothing is his leather jacket.
21. He loves to go to jazz clubs.
22. He's known as the reliable one in the group.
23. His dad is also a musician— and counts as one of his top musical influences.
24. He played celebrity *Who Wants to Be a Millionaire*.
25. He was a psychology major in college.

Scoring

Give yourself one point for every right answer.

Total score, quiz #11: _____

Does anyone but Chris know they're getting their picture taken? Hey guys—over here!

Answers:

1. Joey **2.** Joey **3.** Lance **4.** J.C. **5.** Justin **6.** Chris **7.** J.C. **8.** Justin **9.** J.C. **10.** Lance **11.** Lance **12.** Joey **13.** Chris **14.** Justin **15.** Joey **16.** Lance **17.** Chris **18.** Joey **19.** Chris **20.** J.C. **21.** J.C. **22.** Justin **23.** Joey **24.** Lance **25.** Chris

67

*NSYNC flanks their close friend and fellow performer, Monica.

How Well Do You Know...

J.C.?

J.C. Chasez— babe of babes!

"Being in the studio I get to be creative and I'm the guy that likes jazz, so I have a tendency to take all the songs and make up little jazz versions.... I'm like the sanity in this big mix. Everybody's got their job, and my job is to kind of remind everyone to be on time. I'm the serious one and I like to make sure everything runs smooth." —J.C.

Smooth, yes. Just like that voice. Everyone has their fave *NSYNC-er—for me, it's J.C. There's something about his eyes that gets me every time. Sigh…. Okay, back to reality, Marron! On top of being so luscious and fine, his sexy vocals and sense of responsibility have made him an indispensable member of the group. He had a lot of visibility as one of the senior members of the MMC cast, but that didn't stop him from forging a fast and furious bond with new recruit Justin. And hooray for that, because an *NSYNC without J.C., well, it would just be N Syn (in sin—get it?!)… How well do you know J.C.? Take this quiz and find out!

1. **What's J.C.'s full name?**
   a) Joshua Charlie Chasez
   b) Justin Carlos Chasez
   c) Joshua Scott Chasez
   d) Justin Francesco Chasez

2. **How old was J.C. when he joined the All•New Mickey Mouse Club?**
   a) 13
   b) 15
   c) 17
   d) 19

3. **What was the name of the weekly serial in which J.C. played Clarence "Wipeout" Adams?**
   a) Emerald Cove
   b) Emerald Beach
   c) Glen Cove
   d) Emerald Landing

4. **Where did J.C. grow up?**
   a) Queens, New York
   b) Edgewood, Maryland
   c) Bowie, Maryland
   d) Albany, New York

5. **What's J.C.'s favorite holiday?**
   a) Christmas
   b) Thanksgiving
   c) Easter
   d) Valentine's Day

6. **Who is J.C.'s favorite female singer?**
   a) Britney Spears
   b) Sade
   c) Whitney Houston
   d) Aaliyah

7. **Which of these is not one of J.C.'s nicknames?**
   a) Mr. Casual
   b) Big Daddy
   c) J.C.
   d) Mr. Smoothie

8. **Which of these artists is a musical influence of J.C.'s?**
   a) Sting
   b) Seal
   c) Stevie Wonder
   d) all of the above

9. **Who is J.C.'s favorite model?**
   a) Rebecca Romijn-Stamos
   b) Naomi Campbell
   c) Christy Turlington
   d) Claudia Schiffer

10. **What's J.C.'s father's name?**
    a) Frank
    b) Phil
    c) Rich
    d) Roy

11. **What is J.C.'s sister's name?**
    a) Jennifer
    b) Ashley
    c) Heather
    d) Maria

12. **What's J.C.'s favorite drink?**
    a) seltzer
    b) orange juice
    c) beer
    d) water

13. **J.C.'s favorite color is:**
    a) orange
    b) red
    c) black
    d) blue

14. **What's J.C.'s favorite personal possession?**
    a) his pinky ring
    b) his boxer shorts
    c) his car
    d) his Walkman

15. **J.C.'s favorite football team is:**
    a) the Atlanta Falcons
    b) the New York Giants
    c) the Washington Redskins
    d) the San Francisco 49ers

16. **What's J.C.'s favorite sport?**
    a) football
    b) baseball
    c) basketball
    d) hockey

17. J.C.'s brother's name is:

a) Joshua
b) Frank
c) Tyler
d) Wyatt

18. What's J.C.'s shoe size?

a) 8
b) 10
c) 11
d) 13

19. Which of the following is J.C.'s all-time favorite actress?

a) Cher
b) Jennifer Love Hewitt
c) Bette Davis
d) none of the above

20. What does J.C. miss the most when he's on the road?

a) his mom's home cooking
b) his TV
c) his bed
d) his sound system

21. What's J.C.'s favorite book?

a) <u>The Hobbit</u>, by J.R.R. Tolkien
b) <u>The Backstreet Boys</u>, by Maggie Marron
c) <u>The Firm</u>, by John Grisham
d) <u>Bridget Jones's Diary</u>, by Helen Fielding

22. How do you say J.C.'s last name?

a) CHIZ-IS
b) SHAY-sez
c) SHAZ-ay
d) chaz-EZ

23. What's J.C.'s favorite animated show?

a) <u>The Simpsons</u>
b) <u>South Park</u>
c) <u>The Family Guy</u>
d) <u>Sammy</u>

24. What is J.C. really afraid of?

a) snakes
b) bats
c) needles
d) spiders

25. J.C. says that his everlasting love is:

a) his first-grade teacher
b) his first girlfriend
c) Mickey Mouse
d) none of the above

J.C. on the beach.

Answers:

1) c; 2) b; 3) a; 4) c; 5) a; 6) b; 7) d; 8) d; 9) b; 10) d; 11) c; 12) d; 13) c; 14) d; 15) c; 16) a; 17) c; 18) c; 19) d; 20) c; 21) a; 22) c; 23) b; 24) c; 25) c

Scoring

Give yourself one point for every right answer.

Total score, quiz #12: _____

What an adorable little boy smile he has—especially with those cute cropped bangs!

⊗NSYNC...
and 'N Love

In a recent MTV appearance, Joey announced about himself and the other group members: "We're single and ready to mingle." Well if that's the case, there sure are a lot of us waiting for our chance to mingle! But what are these guys looking for when it comes to romance? What's their history? What do they want for their futures? Read on and find out!

Please be **my** valentine!

Chris says his first date involved dancing at a party with a girl named Kelly. Since then, he's only been in love twice. "The last time was a girl named Catherine," he pines. "It lasted three months and was my longest relationship." Talk about a guy into heavy commitments! Three months as the longest?? He just hasn't found the right person yet!

Chris

What is Chris looking for? His ideal girl will have a great sense of humor and be outgoing—just like him! But will he ever get married? He jokes, "I'll not get married probably, 'cause there isn't any girl who will take me." What is he, crazy?? There's got to be a gazillion gals who would die to give him the honor! What a lunatic. Sheesh!

Joey

Joey doesn't think he's ever truly been in love, but he has had longer relationships than Chris! Joey's first real girlfriend was someone he knew in high school. They broke up when Dinay moved away to go to college, though. Poor Joey!

So what is he looking for in a gal? Well, she has to know how to have fun, she has to have a great personality, and be able to take a joke. And very important to Joey, she has to be honest and real because Joey HATES phonies! He'd love to settle down with a wife and a couple of kids in ten years or so. And while he wants his family to live in a nice home, he really wants to travel around the world with them.

Until then, he'll just keep himself happy with his fantasies. What's the wildest one? "I don't know!" he surmises. "I guess just a big pool of Jell-O—that's all I'm gonna say!" Did I mention that Joey was looking for a woman with a great sense of humor?!?

J.C.

J.C. remembers his first date being at a party: "I met one girl and we danced together. I didn't leave her all night long." Swoon. Sigh. Now get this—his first kiss was in first grade. That naughty little boy!

So what is this eligible bachelor looking for in a woman? Well, while the first thing he may notice about a girl are her eyes and her lips, what he really wants is sincerity over everything else. On his ideal date, he'd take this sincere woman with the gorgeous eyes and lips to dinner and a show. And then a late-night dessert. Now that's romantic.

But silly J.C. says that he's "…not good at being romantic." What?!? "I'm afraid to do things that are too cliché because it's unoriginal, so I don't do a lot of flowers and candy," he explains. "I mean, the best thing I can do is give somebody a nice compliment." Okay, I'll take it!

LANCE Lance still remembers his first kiss. It was with a gal named Bethany Dukes, in kindergarten. Kindergarten?!? What is it with these guys?!?

Lance's ideal girl will be adventurous, fun-loving, affectionate, and let's face it, cute. Like Joey, Lance wants to travel when he gets older—and he also wants to have lots of children and grandchildren!

Justin was a late bloomer by *NSYNC's standards. He shared his first kiss at 10 with his sixth grade girlfriend. "I've always been into older women!" he jokes. **Justin**

If you want to be with Justin, you don't have to be drop-dead gorgeous—but you've gotta have personality! Justin says that "Pretty is cool, but it's not really about looks for me. It's more about personality." He adds: "I like a girl with a good sense of humor, who's humble, and sensitive."

Justin once dated a fan—but he got really burned. Can you imagine? Who could hurt this sweetie?? His first love, that's who. She was an MMC fan who won an invite to an MMC party. He fell head over heels. They dated for nine months—until she cheated on him and broke his heart. Poor Justin admits that it took more than six months for him to get over that!

Despite the rumors, Justin says that he's not romantically involved with Britney Spears, although the two have admitted to sharing a kiss. "When I'm older," Justin says, "I want to be able to look over my shoulder and say with pride that I've done many things in my life." And next to his show-biz career, he'd like to count a wife and children among those accomplishments.

> **Lance and country singer LeAnn Rimes.**

Who the Heck Is That?!? — Part III

By now you should be a pro at this—or are you? Try these questions and see!

1. He can never get enough sleep.
2. His father's name is Randall.
3. He graduated early from high school due to receiving straight As.
4. He was an extra for the closing song of MMC when he met Justin and J.C.
5. He worked for Universal Studios' music and dance group, the Hollywood Hi-Tones.
6. He wears a horseshoe ring and two WWJD (What Would Jesus Do) bracelets given to him by his fans.
7. Until *NSYNC's official fan club was started, his mother stored all of their fan mail in her living room.
8. The singer he admires the most is Stevie Wonder.
9. He introduced the group to the classic song "The Lion Sleeps Tonight," which the guys have since performed in concert.
10. He has a cat named Grendal.
11. His clothing inspires the most laughs with the rest of the group.
12. He collects menus from Hard Rock Cafes all over the world and has almost been able to wallpaper his entire room with them.
13. He attended a very strict Catholic school.
14. His prized possession is an autographed photo of Bruce Lee.
15. He feels taking the job with MMC was one of the smartest decisions he has ever made.
16. He has a bookcase in his house filled with Superman gifts he has received from fans.
17. He has a pet tree named Tree.
18. His biggest flaw is that he tends to be lazy.
19. The guys in the group say he has a fear of commitment when it comes to girls.

20. He loves playing the keyboards and bought a set light enough to take with him on tour.

21. He drives a ruby-red Mercedes-Benz M-class.

22. He loves *I Love Lucy* reruns.

23. He's the joker of the group.

24. He's considered the most serious member of the group.

25. He admits that he got misty-eyed while watching *Titanic*.

*NSYNC at a signing at the Virgin Megastore in New York City.

*NSYNC's larger than life puppets start the show on the <u>No Strings Attached</u> tour.

Answers:

1. J.C. 2. Justin 3. Justin 4. Joey 5. Chris
6. Lance 7. Joey 8. Justin 9. Chris 10. J.C.
11. Joey 12. J.C. 13. J.C. 14. Chris 15. Justin
16. Joey 17. Joey 18. Chris 19. Chris
20. J.C. 21. Justin 22. Lance 23. Chris
24. J.C. 25. Lance

Scoring
Give yourself one point for every right answer.

Total score, quiz #13: _____

*NSYNC: Fact or Fiction—Part III

Ready to dispel more rumors and lies—take this quiz!

1. J.C. hates movies with a lot of action in them. He prefers a good romance.

2. Justin was 10 when he joined the MMC cast.

3. Joey graduated from Dr. Pepper High School in Orlando.

4. Chris's favorite sport is football.

5. The other guys in the band call Lance "Stealth" because he is slow.

6. Chris never graduated from college—he dropped out to join the band.

7. J.C. wears tighty-whiteys!

8. Justin is older than Britney Spears.

9. Lance loves to play basketball.

10. Joey's favorite color is purple.

11. Justin can't get enough junk food.

12. Lance never graduated high school.

13. Chris' most valuable possessions are his Rollerblades and his surfboard.

14. Joey can be very shy and dreads meeting fans and making new friends while he is touring.

15. J.C. was born in Baltimore, Maryland.

16. Justin counts Baby Face among his musical influences.

17. Lance once volunteered to participate in a bullfight.

18. Chris loves chocolate ice cream.

19. Joey is an only child.

20. J.C. won't date a girl unless she's drop-dead gorgeous.

21. Joey's friends with members of 98°.

22. Justin never eats breakfast.

23. Chris loves to drive.

24. Lance loves wearing designer suits—especially Armani!

25. J.C. likes to sing in the shower.

26. J.C. dislikes Chinese food.

27. Lance never drinks coffee.

28. Justin loves snakes and wants to have several of them as pets when he settles down.

29. Chris's favorite actor is Brad Pitt.

30. Joey is an incurable romantic who's been in love more times than he can count.

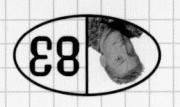

Answers

1. Fiction. These are his favorites. He especially loves the Star Wars trilogy and the Indiana Jones trilogy. 2. Fiction. He was 12. 3. Fiction. It was Dr. Phillips High School, you silly goose! 4. Fact 5. Fiction. They call him Stealth because he sits and watches before he makes his move to meet a girl. 6. Fiction. Chris earned a degree in psychology from Rollins College in Orlando. 7. Fiction. He prefers boxers to briefs—and Tommy Hilfiger boxers at that! 8. Fact 9. Fiction. While he will play, he's not very good and says that the other guys make fun of him! 10. Fact 11. Fiction. Justin actually prefers healthy foods—what a nerd! 12. Fiction. While it is true that he left high school to join *NSYNC, he received his diploma through independent study from the University of Nebraska. 13. Fact 14. Fiction. Nothing could be more false about the member the rest of the guys call "the Flirt." 15. Fiction. While J.C. grew up in Maryland—Bowie—he was actually born in Washington, D.C. 16. Fact 17. Fact—believe it or not! 18. Fact 19. Fiction. He has a sister, Janine, and a brother, Steven. 20. Fiction. J.C. isn't extremely impressed by physical beauty and doesn't like to judge people based on appearance. He'd rather have a gal he can talk to than one he can just look at. 21. Fact 22. Fiction. In fact, he's actually quite grouchy until he eats in the morning. 23. Fiction. Chris doesn't really like to drive. In fact, he doesn't even own a car. Instead, he travels around on a pair of in-line skates! 24. Fiction. Like most of his bandmates, Lance isn't very interested in clothing and prefers to wear jeans or chinos, a T-shirt, and sneakers every day. 25. Fact 26. Totally fiction. J.C. loves Chinese food and eats it at least once a week while on the road! 27. Fiction. In fact, his favorite kind is almond cappuccino. 28. Fiction. Anyone who knows Justin knows he's scared to death of these squirmy animals! 29. Fiction. It's Mel Gibson. 30. Fiction. Joey doesn't think he's ever been in love for real.

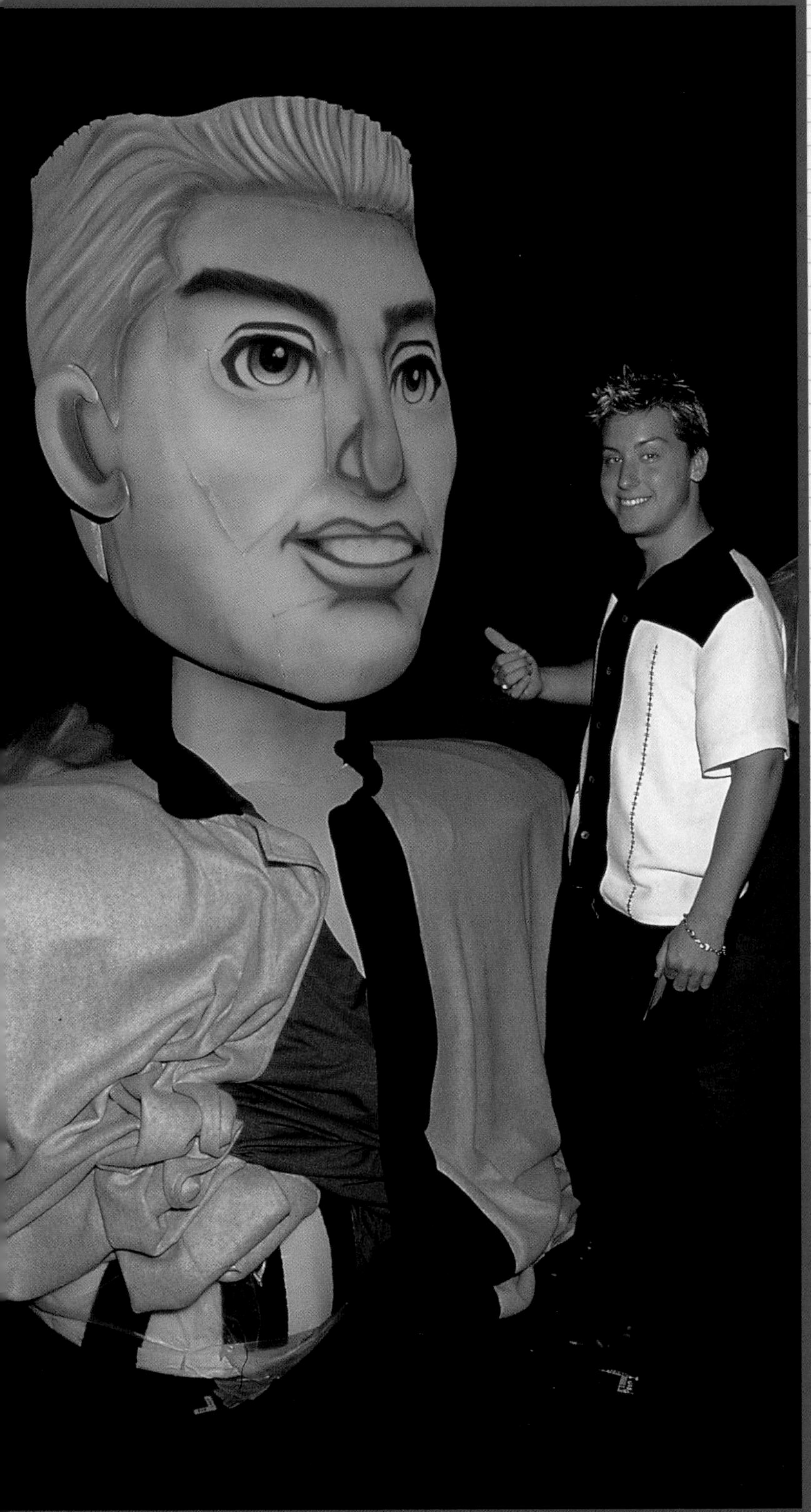

Lance stands next to his puppet to show just how big it really is.

Scoring

Give yourself one point for every right answer.

Total score, quiz #14: ________

BONUS QUIZ!

Well, here's your chance to redeem yourself if you haven't done that well so far—and if you have, well, it's your time to really show off. Good luck!

1. Justin's hobbies include kite flying and skeet shooting.

2. Chris's favorite place on earth is the beach.

3. Justin prefers singing with a backing tape than with a live band because the unpredictability of a live band makes him nervous.

4. Chris graduated from Orlando's Valencia College in 1993 with this member of the Backstreet Boys:

  a) Howie Dorough
  b) Nick Carter
  c) Brian Littrell
  d) A.J. McLean

5. *NSYNC performed this hit single at the American Music Awards on January 17, 2000:

  a) "Tearin' Up My Heart"
  b) "It's Gonna Be Me"
  c) "I Want You Back"
  d) "Bye, Bye, Bye"

6. Lance prefers boxers to briefs.

7. J.C. loves getting dressed up.

8. He started his own line of clothing called Fu-man-skeeto.

9. He says that he's not very good at being romantic.

10. Justin dreads the minutes right before he goes on stage.

11. He says that he is a very spiritual person.

12. He created a charity devoted to improving music education in America's public schools.

13. Lance was born in Clinton, Mississippi.

14. Justin's favorite Disney ride is Space Mountain.

15. *NSYNC has never played mini-concerts in department stores.

16. He says that it would take a lot to make him blush.

17. The most daring thing J.C.'s ever done is:

  a) bungee jump
  b) sky dive
  c) jump off a two-story building
  d) all of the above

18. Chris says that the most common misconception about him is that he is:

  a) stupid
  b) stuck up
  c) shy
  d) mean

19. A big moment for the guys of *NSYNC was presenting this group with their lifetime achievement award:

  a) the BeeGees
  b) the Ramones
  c) the Cure
  d) the Monkees

20. Justin's room at home is filled with 1970s artifacts, incense burners, and funky candles.

21. J.C.'s content just singing and dancing and will probably be doing this for the next 30 years.

22. When MMC was canceled, J.C. embarked on an acting career.

Chris decked out like a matador.

23. Chris was born on October 17, 1974.

24. The group once performed "Bye, Bye, Bye" from the top of a double-decker bus.

25. Justin thinks his worst personality trait is that he's too friendly.

26. On the <u>MMC</u> CD, Justin sings the lead on two songs: "Let's Get Together" and "I Saw Her First."

27. Joey is the only musical member of his family.

28. Two of Lance's hobbies are playing video games and weight training.

29. Justin wears boxer shorts by Tommy Hilfiger.

30. He says that he has always loved football and that as a child he had a little football to suck on instead of a pacifier.

31. His greatest fear is heights.

32. His greatest fear is things that buzz.

33. J.C. says that the secret to his success is:

a) hard work
b) persistence
c) dedication
d) all of the above

34. Lance's favorite feature is:

a) his arms
b) his legs
c) his eyes
d) his hair

35. Joey compares the group's success to Mr. Toad's Wild Ride at Disney World because:

a) it makes them dizzy
b) it just keeps going
c) there are a lot of ups and downs
d) all of the above

36. He played the lead role in his high school production of <u>Oliver</u>.

37. He is very superstitious.

38. He has four half-sisters.

39. He loves to tap dance.

40. The shade of dye Joey used to get his brilliant red hair is called:

a) Red Corvette
b) Candy Apple Red
c) Red Hot
d) Fire Engine Red

Answers

1. Fiction. His love is his work. When he isn't working, he counts singing and dancing as his main hobbies! **2.** Fact **3.** Fiction. Justin actually thrives on the unpredictable nature of a live performance. He finds it very exciting. **4.** a **5.** b **6.** d **7.** Fact **7.** Fiction. J.C. doesn't like getting dressed up at all. In fact, he's happiest wearing jeans, sneakers, and an old sweater over a T-shirt. **8.** Chris **9.** J.C. **10.** Fiction. Justin lives for the adrenaline rush he gets right before he hits the boards. **11.** Justin **12.** Justin **13.** Fiction. Lance was born in Laurel, Mississippi, and moved to Clinton with his family at the age of 11. **14.** Fact **15.** Fiction. They've performed the mall circuit, including doing shows at Macy's in New York, Boston, and Atlanta. **16.** J.C. **17.** c **18.** b **19.** a **20.** Fact **21.** Fiction. Actually, every aspect of the music industry fascinates J.C., from writing songs to producing. In fact, J.C. writes a lot of songs and hopes *NSYNC will write all of their own music someday. He also wouldn't mind having an acting career! **22.** Fiction. When the show was canceled, he began to make plans for a solo singing career—until he hooked up with the other guys, that is! **23.** Fiction. He was born in 1971. **24.** Fiction. It was "Tearin' Up My Heart"! **25.** Fiction. It's that he's too impatient and he procrastinates! **26.** Fiction, it's J.C.! **27.** Fiction. Joey's father used to belong to a singing group called the Orions, and Joey's sister, Janine, is also a singer. Their brother, Steven, is a dancer for a group called Solid Harmonie. **28.** Fact **29.** Fiction. He just loves his Calvin Klein briefs. **30.** Chris **31.** Chris **32.** Lance **33.** d **34.** c **35.** b **36.** Chris **37.** Chris **38.** Chris **39.** Joey **40.** a

Scoring

Give yourself one point for every right answer.

Total score, Bonus Quiz: _____

Aha! So Mickey was the mysterious fifth member of the band before Lance came along!

What's Your Total Score?

Now that you've reached the end of the book, it's time to find out just what kind of a fan you are. Total up your scores for all the quizzes in the book:

Quiz #1:

Quiz #2:

Quiz #3:

Quiz #4:

Quiz #5:

Quiz #6:

Quiz #7:

Quiz #8:

Quiz #9:

Quiz #10:

Quiz #11:

Quiz #12:

Quiz #13:

Quiz #14:

Bonus quiz:

Total Score:

How Big an *NSYNC Fan Are You?!?!?
Compare your points below and find out!

301-400 points

Excellent! You are the hands-down winner. You've earned the top grade: an A. Way to go! Now, if you didn't get exactly 400 points, you still have a thing or two to learn, which actually only means more fun for you. After all, it's not like it's torture to visit the website daily, or comb through every magazine out there for more and more facts, or make it a point to listen to their CDs at least twice a day, now is it?

Surf's up for these huge 1999 Teen Choice Awards winners!

201-300 points

Not too shabby. While you know a lot about the guys, you now have the chance to get to know them better. Have you checked out the official bio yet? Maybe you can read that book with a bunch of friends at the mall. Better yet, why not host a sleepover party with an *NSYNC theme. During the night, exchange scrapbooks, albums, magazine articles, tidbits of info you've picked up over the years—then get an hour or so of sleep! In the morning, you can all take the quiz together and see how you do. You'll be a pro in no time—and you'll also be helping out your friends!

101-200 points

Hmmm. Only so-so. You probably love looking at and listening to the guys so much that you haven't really had time yet to learn as much as you possibly can about them. Okay, well here's what you should do. Hang your posters on one wall in your room. Now, sit in a chair with your back facing that wall (and don't try any funny business with mirrors or anything!!) and crack open a few of the books. Remember: the more you know about them, the better you'll understand them, and the more you'll truly love them. Now get reading! Come on—go!

0-100 points

Oh no! Not great. You have a whole lot to learn about the boys of *NSYNC, girlfriend. Perhaps you've just discovered this heavenly quintet. Maybe you took this quiz prematurely. Maybe you're so fixated on one of the guys that you haven't had a chance to learn about the others yet… Whatever the reason, it's time to educate yourself! Read all the books out there about *NSYNC. Visit the website regularly. Watch all the specials. After a month of cramming, come back and take the quiz again and see how you do!

Um, looking for some spare change?

⊗NSYNC Resource List

⊗NSYNC Fan Club

The *NSYNC Official
    International Fan Club
P.O. Box 5248
Belingham, Washington 98227
USA

Contact:
    Gerri Karr, Fan Club Manager

Websites

Official: www.nsync.com
Also worth a visit:
    http://www.angelfire.com/il/
        laurennlance/index.html
    www.angelfire.com/music/
        nsyncplaza/
    www.angelfire.com/ne/
        getsikedwithnsync/
    www.billboard.com
    www.nsyncheaven.com
    www.rollingstone.com
    www.travel.to/n_sync/
    www.wallofsound.go.com

There's lots more where that came from. Your best bet is to go to one of your favorite search engines, like Yahoo or Lycos, type in "n sync," and a whole world of *NSYNC information will be open to you. Here's a tip: log on with your 'rents when you want to search this stuff out. There's a lot of phony baloney on the Web and your folks can help you get past all that and into the good stuff!

Magazines

Check out these magazines monthly for stories and interviews featuring your favorite boy band!

All-Stars
B.B.
Blast
Cosmo Girl!
Cute
Entertainment Teen
J – 14
Jane
Kickin'
Seventeen
Sixteen
Super Teen
Teen Beat
Teen Celebrity
Teen People

Bibliography

Periodicals
Christman, Ed and Anna Berent. "Jive's 'N Sync Breaks Records." *Billboard.* (April 1, 2000): 1.

Gadzik, Tanya. "Oxy Balance Gets 'N Sync With Teens." *Brandweek.* (February 15, 1999): 12.

Helligar, Jeremy. "Boy Power: Watch Your Backs, Backstreet Boys! 'N Sync conquers charts—and teenage hearts—with sweet harmonies." *People Weekly.* (February 8, 1999): 93.

"Last Week's Answer: The U.S. Virgin Islands." *Time for Kids.* (December 18, 1998): 8.

Laudadio, Marisa. "Catching Up With Justin Timberlake of 'N Sync." *Teen Magazine.* (January 2000): 46.

Laudadio, Marisa. "The Making of 'N Sync's newest video." *Teen Magazine.* (April 2000): 72.

Marron, Maggie. "N Sync." *Kickin'.* (vol 2 no 3).

Paoletta, Michael. "Jive's Plan: 'N Sync Everywhere." *Billboard.* (February 19, 2000): 1.

Pesselnick, Jill. "April Certs Mark Feats By 'N Sync, Dion, Chicks." *Billboard.* (May 13, 2000): 137.

Taylor, Chuck. "'N Sync Spends Its 'Time' Evolving Into More Than Just a Teen Pop Sensation." *Billboard.* (November 7, 1998): 104.

Waddell, Ray. "'N Sync In Rhythm: $30 Mil Year Possible For Youth Band." *Amusement Business.* (February 1, 1999): 3.

World Wide Web

"'N Sync Expands Horizons With Alabama, Gloria Estefan." *Mtv.com*

"N Sync." *launch.com*

"Which Star Signs Are Compatible?" *www.stargazers.com*

agirlsworld.com

Gelman, Jason. "Estefan on 'Music' and 'N Sync." *launch.com*

nsync.com

ymshomepage.com

Books

'N Sync Backstreet Pass: Your Kickin' Keepsake Scrapbook. Scholastic: New York. 1999.

Nichols, Angie. *'N Sync: Get 'N Sync With the Guys.* Billboard: New York. 1998.

Photo Credits

Archive Photos: © Reuters / Sam Mircovich: pp. 68-69; © Reuters / Fred Prouser: pp. 84-85; © Reuters/ Rose Prouser: p. 33

Globe Photos, Inc.: © Fitzroy Barrett: p. 27; © Kelly Jordan: pp. 20, 51, 77; © Milan Ryba: p. 26; © Walter Weissman: pp. 64 Bottom, 65, 79

Courtesy of Jive: © Mark Seliger: pp. 94-95

London Features Int'l Ltd.: © Anthony Cutajar: pp. 24-25, 30, 37, 40 Bottom, 63, Justin page number icons; © Gregg DeGuire: pp. 90-91; © John James: p. 89; © Jen Lowery: pp. 38-39, 52; © Ilpo Musto: pp. 40 Top, 41 Bottom; © Dennis Van Tine: pp. 41 Top, 64 Top, Lance page number icons; © Ron Wolfson: pp. 57, 80-81, 83

Photofest: pp. 34-35

Retna Ltd.: © Bob Berg: p. 14; © Lillian Bonomo: p. 87; © Bill Davila: p.67; © Melanie Edwards: p. 70; © Tim Hale: p. 3; © Bernhard Kuhmstedt: pp. 2, 6-7, 10, 11, 16, 17, 22-23, 31, 36, 41 Middle, 44, 45, 48, 49, 50, 53, 54, 55, 58-59, 62, 72, 73, Joey page number icons, Chris page number icons, J.C. page number icons; © Sam Levi: pp. 18-19; © Neal Preston: p. 47; © Call/ Redferns: pp. 9, 42, 60; © John Spellman: p. 56; © Kelly A. Swift: pp. 12-13; © Nick Tansley/ All Action: pp. 28, 74, 92